TED
HUGHES

*Moortown
Diary*

faber and faber

Moortown first published in 1979
by Faber and Faber Limited
3 Queen Square London WC1N 3AU

This selection of poems from
Moortown with notes first published in
this edition in 1989

Phototypeset by Wilmaset, Birkenhead, Wirral
Printed and bound in Great Britain by
TJ International Ltd, Padstow, Cornwall

A CIP record for this book
is available from the British Library

ISBN 0-571-23180-2
ISBN 978-0-571-23180-5

1 3 5 7 9 10 8 6 4 2

Contents

In memory of Jack Orchard

Preface

In the early 1970s my wife and I bought a small farm just
north of the northern edge of Dartmoor, in what is
generally known as North Devon, and farmed it in
partnership with her father, Jack Orchard, to whom I
have dedicated this book. He was a retired farmer whose
family had farmed in Devon for generations. My own
experience of farming had previously been limited to
playing and working on farms in West and South
Yorkshire when I was a boy, just failing to buy a farm in
Australia when I left University, and since then rearing
the occasional bullock or two. My mother's mother's
family had farmed in West Yorkshire, so I always heard
the common saying 'back to the land in three gen-
erations' with a cocked ear. However it was, when the
opportunity to buy a farm suddenly came, I took it. We
had no idea what an interesting moment we had chosen.

Even then, in the early 1970s, the ancient farming
community in North Devon was still pretty intact and
undisturbed, more so than anywhere else in England.
No industrial development or immigrant population had
ever disrupted it. A lucky combination of factors kept
tourists to the minimum, and those few to the sparse
resorts on the rocky fringe. The high rainfall and poor
soil deterred the sort of farmer who might try to change
things. Cut off by Exmoor to the east, Dartmoor to the
south, and that northern coastline of high, wreckers' cliff
in which the only harbourage was all but closed by a
dangerous bar, North Devon felt like an island. The rest
of England had always ignored it. And there was a
palpable feeling here that England (along with South
Devon and Cornwall) was another country and could be

vii

ignored in return. Over the centuries this has bred a curious mentality. Yorkshire farmers are thought to be an independent lot, and those I knew certainly were, but even fifty years ago they were embattled, alert to all the buffeting modern pressures of mass population and industry. The isolated self-sufficiency of the old North Devon farmers was something else altogether, like nothing I had ever encountered.

Buried in their deep valleys, in undateable cob-walled farms hidden not only from the rest of England but even from each other, connected by the inexplicable, Devonshire, high-banked, deep-cut lanes that are more like a defence-maze of burrows, these old Devonians lived in a time of their own. It was common to hear visitors say: 'Everything here's in another century!' But what they really meant, maybe, was that all past centuries were still very present here, wide-open, unchanged, unexorcized, and potent enough to overwhelm any stray infiltrations of modernity. The farmers lived lightly in the day and the year, but heavily in that long backward perspective of their ancient landscape and their homes. The breed was so distinct, so individualized and all of a piece, they seemed to me almost a separate race. I could believe they were still that Celtic tribe the Romans had known as the *Dumnoni*, 'the people of the deep valleys', a confederacy of petty kings, hidden in their strongholds that were only just beginning to emerge out of the old oak forest.

How rapidly that changed within the next decade, how completely that ancient world and its spirit vanished, as the older generation died off and gave way to sons who were plunged into the financial nightmares, the technological revolutions and international market madness that have devastated farmers, farms and farming ever since, intensifying right up to this moment, is no part of what I recorded in the passages of verse collected here. Or it is only a small, indirect part, in so far as my wife and I inevitably belonged, in many respects, to the new wave. Against the strong resistance of her father we did try some of the novelties, lusted after the exotic, foreign breeds of cattle that poured into England during the 1970s, boosted our palpitations on the regular sales blast of *Farmer's Weekly*, with its dazing propaganda for new chemicals, new machinery, more chemicals, new methods, different chemicals, new gimmicks, new short-cuts, every possible new way of wringing that critical extra per cent out of the acreage and the animals. We were dragged, as bewildered as the rest, into that seismic upheaval which has been, probably, one of the biggest extinctions so far in the evolution of English countryside and farming tradition. Few farmers understood what was happening. Within a very short time the last vestige of grandeur in the real work had vanished, the product itself had become a weirdly scandalous, unwanted surplus, the livestock a danger to public health (and nobody knew better than the farmer what he pumped into them), the very soil a kind of poison, the rivers sewers. This deeply satisfying, self-reliant if occasionally gruelling way of life had mutated – into a jittery, demoralized, industrial servitude, in effect farming not stock and land but grants and subsidies, at the mercy of foreign politicians, big business conglomerates, bank managers and accountants. A sharp nose for these things soon enlightened us, and we settled into the old-fashioned routine of running a suckler herd of beef cows, a flock of breeding ewes, and keeping everything going on bailer twine.

Even so, whether we liked it or not, we were in the front line of the first campaign of what felt very much like the Third World War conducted by other means – the EEC Agricultural Policy War. At one point, while we were trying to sell some of the animals I mention in these pages, cattle-market prices dropped as low as ever in history. Buying a steak at a butcher's shop you would not have noticed the tremor in the scales, but at that time a farmer sold a calf and with the proceeds managed to buy a Mars Bar; a local farmer leaving Hatherleigh Market found two unfamiliar calves in his trailer – dumped there by the owner who could neither get a price for them nor afford to take them back home and feed them.

The pieces in this collection came about by the way. It occurred to me from time to time that interesting things were happening, and that I ought to make a note of them, a note of the details in particular, partly with the idea of maybe using them at some future time in a piece of writing, and partly to make a fleeting snapshot, for myself, of a precious bit of my life. Over those first years, as the evidence now shows me, that impulse came to me about forty times. And most of the results are here.

I should say something about the form and style in which these pieces are written. I set them down in what appears to be verse for a simple reason. In making a note about anything, if I wish to look closely I find I can move closer, and stay closer, if I phrase my observations about it in rough lines. So these improvised verses are nothing more than this: my own way of getting reasonably close to what is going on, and staying close, and of excluding everything else that might be pressing to interfere with the watching eye. In a sense, the method excludes the poetic process as well.

This sort of thing had to be set down soon after the event. If I missed the moment – which meant letting a night's sleep intervene before I took up a pen – I could always see quite clearly what had been lost. By the next day, the processes of 'memory', the poetic process, had already started. Though all the details were still absolutely fresh, most of them no longer seemed essential to the new pattern taking control. The pieces here which begin to look a little more like 'poems' mark the occasions where I had 'missed the moment' in this way.

I regarded them as casual journal notes, and made no attempt to do anything with them, until one day a magazine editor asked me for a poem. Thinking I might find something to work on, I then looked these pieces over, and picked out 'February 17th'. It didn't take me long to realize that I was in the position of a translator: whatever I might make of this passage, I was going to have to destroy the original. And what was original here was not some stranger's poem but the video and surviving voice-track of one of my own days, a moment of my life that I did not want to lose. I then saw that all the other entries, even the more diffuse, still carried that same souvenir bloom for me. Altering any word felt like retouching an old home movie with new bits of fake-original voice and fake-original actions.

I put them together for my wife, as a memorial to her father. For any other reader who might find something of interest in them I have added a few sentences of introductory context here and there, as I would if I were reading them to an audience.

Rain

Rain. Floods. Frost. And after frost, rain.
Dull roof-drumming. Wraith-rain pulsing across
  purple-bare woods
Like light across heaved water. Sleet in it.
And the poor fields, miserable tents of their hedges.
Mist-rain off-world. Hills wallowing
In and out of a grey or silvery dissolution. A farm
  gleaming,
Then all dull in the near drumming. At field-corners
Brown water backing and brimming in grass.
Toads hop across rain-hammered roads. Every
  mutilated leaf there
Looks like a frog or a rained-out mouse. Cattle
Wait under blackened backs. We drive post-holes.
They half fill with water before the post goes in.
Mud-water spurts as the iron bar slam-burns
The oak stake-head dry. Cows
Tamed on the waste mudded like a rugby field
Stand and watch, come very close for company
In the rain that goes on and on, and gets colder.
They sniff the wire, sniff the tractor, watch. The
  hedges
Are straggles of gap. A few haws. Every half-ton cow
Sinks to the fetlock at every sliding stride.
They are ruining their field and they know it.
They look out sideways from under their brows which
  are
Their only shelter. The sunk scrubby wood
Is a pulverized wreck, rain riddles its holes
To the drowned roots. A pheasant looking black
In his waterproofs, bends at his job in the stubble.

The mid-afternoon dusk soaks into
The soaked thickets. Nothing protects them.
The fox corpses lie beaten to their bare bones,
Skin beaten off, brains and bowels beaten out.
Nothing but their blueprint bones last in the rain,
Sodden soft. Round their hay racks, calves
Stand in a shine of mud. The gateways
Are deep obstacles of mud. The calves look up,
    through plastered forelocks,
Without moving. Nowhere they can go
Is less uncomfortable. The brimming world
And the pouring sky are the only places
For them to be. Fieldfares squeal over, sodden
Toward the sodden wood. A raven,
Cursing monotonously, goes over fast
And vanishes in rain-mist. Magpies
Shake themselves hopelessly, hop in the spatter.
    Misery.
Surviving green of ferns and brambles is tumbled
Like an abandoned scrapyard. The calves
Wait deep beneath their spines. Cows roar
Then hang their noses to the mud.
Snipe go over, invisible in the dusk,
With their squelching cries.

4 December 1973

2

Dehorning

Bad-tempered bullying bunch, the horned cows
Among the unhorned. Feared, spoilt.
Cantankerous at the hay, at assemblies, at crowded
Yard operations. Knowing their horn-tips' position
To a fraction, every other cow knowing it too,
Like their own tenderness. Horning of bellies, hair-
    tufting
Of horn-tips. Handy levers. But
Off with the horns.
So there they all are in the yard –
The pick of the bullies, churning each other
Like thick fish in a bucket, churning their mud.
One by one, into the cage of the crush: the needle,
A roar not like a cow – more like a tiger,
Blast of air down a cavern, and long, long
Beginning in pain and ending in terror – then the
    next.
The needle between the horn and the eye, so deep
Your gut squirms for the eyeball twisting
In its pink-white fastenings of tissue. This side and
    that.
Then the first one anaesthetized, back in the crush.
The bulldog pincers in the septum, stretched full
    strength,
The horn levered right over, the chin pulled round
With the pincers, the mouth drooling, the eye
Like a live eye caught in a pan, like the eye of a fish
Imprisoned in air. Then the cheese cutter
Of braided wire, and stainless steel peg handles,
Aligned on the hair-bedded root of the horn, then
    leaning

3

Backward full weight, pull-punching backwards,
Left right left right and the blood leaks
Down over the cheekbone, the wire bites
And buzzes, the ammonia horn-burn smokes
And the cow groans, roars shapelessly, hurls
Its half-ton commotion in the tight cage. Our faces
Grimace like faces in the dentist's chair. The horn
Rocks from its roots, the wire pulls through
The last hinge of hair, the horn is heavy and free,
And a water-pistol jet of blood
Rains over the one who holds it – a needle jet
From the white-rasped and bloody skull-crater. Then
    tweezers
Twiddle the artery nozzle, knotting it enough,
And purple antiseptic squirts a cuttlefish cloud over it.
Then the other side the same. We collect
A heap of horns. The floor of the crush
Is a trampled puddle of scarlet. The purple-crowned
    cattle,
The bullies, with suddenly no horns to fear,
Start ramming and wrestling. Maybe their heads
Are still anaesthetized. A new order
Among the hornless. The bitchy high-headed
Straight-back brindle, with her Spanish bull trot,
And her head-shaking snorting advance and her crazy
    spirit,
Will have to get maternal. What she's lost
In weapons, she'll have to make up for in tits.
But they've all lost one third of their beauty.

14 May 1974

4

Poor birds

In the boggy copse. Blue
Dusk presses into their skulls
Electrodes of stars. All night
Clinging to sodden twigs, with twiggy claws,
They dream the featherless, ravenous
Machinery of heaven. At dawn, fevered,
They flee to the field. All day
They try to get some proper sleep without
Losing sight of the grass. Panics
Fling them from hill to hill. They search everywhere
For the safety that sleeps
Everywhere in the closed faces
Of stones.

10 December 1973

Feeding out-wintering cattle at twilight

The wind is inside the hill.
The wood is a struggle – like a wood
Struggling through a wood. A panic
Only just holds off – every gust
Breaches the sky-walls and it seems, this time,
The whole sea of air will pour through,
The thunder will take deep hold, roots
Will have to come out, every loose thing
Will have to lift and go. And the cows, dark lumps of
    dusk
Stand waiting, like nails in a tin roof.
For the crucial moment, taking the strain
In their stirring stillness. As if their hooves
Held their field in place, held the hill
To its trembling shape. Night-thickness
Purples in the turmoil, making
Everything more alarming. Unidentifiable, tiny
Birds go past like elf-bolts.
Battling the hay-bales from me, the cows
Jostle and crush, like hulls blown from their moorings
And piling at the jetty. The wind
Has got inside their wintry buffalo skins,
Their wild woolly bulk-heads, their fierce, joyful
    breathings
And the reckless strength of their necks.
What do they care, their hooves
Are knee-deep in porridge of earth –
The hay blows luminous tatters from their chewings,
A fiery loss, frittering downwind,
Snatched away over the near edge
Where the world becomes water

Thundering like a flood-river at night.
They grunt happily, half-dissolved
On their steep, hurtling brink, as I flounder back
Towards headlights.

17 February 1974

Foxhunt

Two days after Xmas, near noon, as I listen
The hounds behind the hill
Are changing ground, a cloud of excitements,
Their voices like rusty, reluctant
Rolling stock being shunted. The hunt
Has tripped over a fox
At the threshold of the village. A crow in the fir
Is inspecting his nesting site, and he expostulates
At the indecent din. A blackbird
Starts up its cat-alarm. The grey-cloud mugginess
Of the year in its pit trying to muster
Enough energy to start opening again
Roars distantly. Everything sodden. The fox
Is flying, taking his first lesson
From the idiot pack-noise, the puppyish whine-yelps
Curling up like hounds' tails, and the gruff military
    barkers:
A machine with only two products:
Dog-shit and dead foxes. Lorry engines
As usual modulating on the main street hill
Complicate the air, and the fox runs in a suburb
Of indifferent civilized noises. Now the yelpings
Enrich their brocade, thickening closer
In the maze of wind-currents. The orchards
And the hedges stand in coma. The pastures
Have got off so far lightly, are firm, cattle
Still nose hopefully, as if spring might be here
Missing out winter. Big lambs
Are organizing their gangs in gateways. The fox
Hangs his silver tongue in the world of noise
Over his spattering paws. Will he run

Till his muscles suddenly turn to iron,
Till blood froths his mouth as his lungs tatter,
Till his feet are raw blood-sticks and his tail
Trails thin as a rat's? Or will he
Make a mistake, jump the wrong way, jump right
Into the hound's mouth? As I write this down
He runs still fresh, with all his chances before him.

27 December 1975

New Year exhilaration

On the third day
Finds its proper weather. Pressure
Climbing and the hard blue sky
Scoured by gales. The world's being
Swept clean. Twigs that can't cling
Go flying, last leaves ripped off
Bowl along roads like daring mice. Imagine
The new moon hightide sea under this
Rolling of air-weights. Exhilaration
Lashes everything. Windows flash,
White houses dazzle, fields glow red.
Seas pour in over the land, invisible maelstroms
Set the house-joints creaking. Every twig-end
Writes its circles and the earth
Is massaged with roots. The powers of hills
Hold their bright faces in the wind-shine.
The hills are being honed. The river
Thunders like a factory, its weirs
Are tremendous engines. People
Walk precariously, the whole landscape
Is imperilled, like a tarpaulin
With the wind under it. 'It nearly
Blew me up the chymbley!' And a laugh
Blows away like a hat.

3 January 1975

Struggle

We had been expecting her to calve
And there she was, just after dawn, down.
Private, behind bushed hedge-cuttings, in a low rough
   corner.
The walk towards her was like a walk into danger,
Caught by her first calf, the small-boned black and
   white heifer
Having a bad time. She lifted her head,
She reached for us with a wild, flinging look
And flopped flat again. There was the calf,
White-faced, lion-coloured, enormous, trapped
Round the waist by his mother's purpled elastic,
His heavy long forelegs limply bent in a not-yet-
   inherited gallop,
His head curving up and back, pushing for the udder
Which had not yet appeared, his nose scratched and
   reddened
By an ill-placed clump of bitten-off rushes,
His fur dried as if he had been
Half-born for hours, as he probably had.
Then we heaved on his forelegs,
And on his neck, and half-born he mooed
Protesting about everything. Then bending him down,
Between her legs, and sliding a hand
Into the hot tunnel, trying to ease
His sharp hip-bones past her pelvis,
Then twisting him down, so you expected
His spine to slip its sockets,
And one hauling his legs, and one embracing his wet
   waist
Like pulling somebody anyhow from a bog,

And one with hands easing his hips past the corners
Of his tunnel mother, till something gave.
The cow flung her head and lifted her upper hind leg
With every heave and something gave
Almost a click –
And his scrubbed wet enormous flanks came sliding
    out,
Coloured ready for the light his incredibly long hind
    legs
From the loose red flapping sack-mouth
Followed by a gush of colours, a mess
Of puddled tissues and jellies.
He mooed feebly and lay like a pieta Christ
In the cold easterly daylight. We dragged him
Under his mother's nose, her stretched-out exhausted
    head,
So she could get to know him with lickings.
They lay face to face like two mortally wounded
    duellists.
We stood back, letting the strength flow towards
    them.
We gave her a drink, we gave her hay. The calf
Started his convalescence
From the gruelling journey. All day he lay
Overpowered by limpness and weight.
We poured his mother's milk into him
But he had not strength to swallow.
He made a few clumsy throat gulps, then lay
Mastering just breathing.
We took him inside. We tucked him up
In front of a stove, and tried to pour
Warm milk and whisky down his throat and not into
    his lungs.
But his eye just lay suffering the monstrous weight of
    his head,

The impossible job of his marvellous huge limbs.
He could not make it. He died called Struggle.
Son of Patience.

17 April 1974

Bringing in new couples

Wind out of freezing Europe. A mean snow
Fiery cold. Ewes caked crusty with snow,
Their new hot lambs wet trembling
And crying on trampled patches, under the hedge –
Twenty miles of open lower landscape
Blows into their wetness. The field smokes and
    writhes
Burning like a moor with snow-fumes.
Lambs nestling to make themselves comfortable
While the ewe nudges and nibbles at them
And the numbing snow-wind blows on the blood
    tatters
At her breached back-end.
The moor a grey sea-shape. The wood
Thick-fingered density, a worked wall of whiteness.
The old sea-roar, sheep-shout, lamb-wail.
Redwings needling invisible. A fright
Smoking among trees, the hedges blocked.
Lifting of ice-heavy ewes, trampling anxieties
As they follow their wide-legged tall lambs,
Tripods craning to cry bewildered.
We coax the mothers to follow their babies
And they do follow, running back
In sudden convinced panic to the patch
Where the lamb had been born, dreading
She must have been deceived away from it
By crafty wolvish humans, then coming again
Defenceless to the bleat she's attuned to
And recognizing her own – a familiar
Detail in the meaningless shape-mass

14

Of human arms, legs, body-clothes – her lamb on the
    white earth
Held by those hands. Then vanishing again
Lifted. Then only the disembodied cry
Going with the human, while she runs in a circle
On the leash of the cry. While the wind
Presses outer space into the grass
And alarms wrens deep in brambles
With hissing fragments of stars.

16 February 1975

Snow smoking as the fields boil

The bull weeps.
The trough solidifies.
The cock pheasant has forgotten his daughters.
The fox crosses mid-field, careless of acquittal.
Twigs cannot pay the interest.
The farm-roofs sink in the welter again, like a whale's
    fluke.
Sheep fade humbly.
The owl cries early, breaking parole,
With icicles darkening witness.

8 February 1975

Tractor

The tractor stands frozen – an agony
To think of. All night
Snow packed its open entrails. Now a head-pincering
    gale,
A spill of molten ice, smoking snow,
Pours into its steel.
At white heat of numbness it stands
In the aimed hosing of ground-level fieriness.

It defies flesh and won't start.
ands are like wounds already
Inside armour gloves, and feet are unbelievable
As if the toe-nails were all just torn off.
I stare at it in hatred. Beyond it
The copse hisses – capitulates miserably
In the fleeing, failing light. Starlings,
A dirtier sleetier snow, blow smokily, unendingly,
    over
Towards plantations eastward.
All the time the tractor is sinking
Through the degrees, deepening
Into its hell of ice.

The starter lever
Cracks its action, like a snapping knuckle.
The battery is alive – but like a lamb
Trying to nudge its solid-frozen mother –
While the seat claims my buttock-bones, bites
With the space-cold of earth, which it has joined
In one solid lump.

I squirt commercial sure-fire
Down the black throat – it just coughs.
It ridicules me – a trap of iron stupidity
I've stepped into. I drive the battery
As if I were hammering and hammering
The frozen arrangement to pieces with a hammer
And it jabbers laughing pain-crying mockingly
Into happy life.

And stands
Shuddering itself full of heat, seeming to enlarge
   slowly
Like a demon demonstrating
A more-than-usually-complete materialization –
Suddenly it jerks from its solidarity
With the concrete, and lurches towards a stanchion
Bursting with superhuman well-being and abandon
Shouting Where Where?

Worse iron is waiting. Power-lift kneels,
Levers awake imprisoned deadweight,
Shackle-pins bedded in cast-iron cow-shit.
The blind and vibrating condemned obedience
Of iron to the cruelty of iron,
Wheels screeched out of their night-locks –

Fingers
Among the tormented
Tonnage and burning of iron

Eyes
Weeping in the wind of chloroform

And the tractor, streaming with sweat,
Raging and trembling and rejoicing.

31 January 1976

Roe-deer

In the dawn-dirty light, in the biggest snow of the year
Two blue-dark deer stood in the road, alerted.

They had happened into my dimension
The moment I was arriving just there.

They planted their two or three years of secret
   deerhood
Clear on my snow-screen vision of the abnormal

And hesitated in the all-way disintegration
And stared at me. And so for some lasting seconds

I could think the deer were waiting for me
To remember the password and sign

That the curtain had blown aside for a moment
And there where the trees were no longer trees, nor
   the road a road

The deer had come for me.

Then they ducked through the hedge, and upright
   they rode their legs
Away downhill over a snow-lonely field

Towards tree dark – finally
Seeming to eddy and glide and fly away up

Into the boil of big flakes.
The snow took them and soon their nearby hoofprints
    as well

Revising its dawn inspiration
Back to the ordinary.

13 February 1973

Couples under cover

The ewes are in the shed
Under clapping wings of corrugated iron
Where entering rays of snow cut horizontal
Fiery and radio-active, a star-dust.
The oaks outside, half-digested
With a writhing white fire-snow off the hill-field
Burning to frails of charcoal
Roar blind, and swing blindly, a hill-top
Helpless self-defence. Snow
Is erasing them, whitening blanks
Against a dirty whiteness. The new jolly lambs
Are pleased with their nursery. A few cavorts
Keep trying their hind-legs – up and a twist,
So they stagger back to balance, bewildered
By the life that's working at them. Heads, safer,
Home in on udders, under-groin hot flesh-tent,
Hide eyes in muggy snugness. The ewes can't settle,
Heads bony and ratty with anxiety,
Keyed to every wind-shift, light-footed
To leap clear when the hill-top
Starts to peel off, or those tortured tree-oceans
Come blundering through the old stonework.
They don't appreciate the comfort.
They'd as soon be in midfield suffering
The twenty mile snow-gale of unprotection,
Ice-balls anaesthetizing their back-end blood-tatters,
Watching and worrying while a lamb grows stranger –
A rumpy-humped skinned-looking rabbit
Whose hunger no longer works.

                              One day
Of slightly unnatural natural comfort, and the lambs
Will toss out into the snow, imperishable
Like trawlers, bobbing in gangs, while the world
Welters unconscious into whiteness.

                                    4 March 1974

Surprise

Looking at cows in their high-roofy roomy
Windy home, mid-afternoon idling,
Late winter, near spring, the fields not greening,
The wind North-East and sickening, the hay
Shrinking, the year growing. The parapets
Of toppled hay, the broken walls of hay,
The debris of hay. The peace of cattle
Mid-afternoon, cud-munching, eyelids lowered.
The deep platform of dung. Looking at cows
Sharing their trance, it was an anomalous
Blue plastic apron I noticed
Hitched under the tail of one cow
That went on munching, with angling ears. A
    glistening
Hanging sheet of blue-black. I thought
Of aprons over ewes' back-ends
To keep the ram out till it's timely. I thought
Of surgical aprons to keep cleanliness
Under the shit-fall. Crazily far thoughts
Proposed themselves as natural, and I almost
Looked away. Suddenly
The apron slithered, and a whole calf's
Buttocks and hind-legs – whose head and forefeet
Had been hidden from me by another cow –
Toppled out of its mother, and collapsed on the
    ground.
Leisurely, as she might be leisurely curious,
She turned, pulling her streamers of blood-tissue
Away from this lumpish jetsam. She nosed it
Where it lay like a still-birth in its tissues.
She began to nibble and lick. The jelly

Shook its head and nosed the air. She gave it
The short small swallowed moo-grunts hungry cows
Give when they stand suddenly among plenty.

21 March 1975

Last night

She would not leave her dead twins. The whole flock
Went on into the next field, over the hill,
But she stayed with her corpses. We took one
And left one to keep her happy.
The North wind brought the worst cold
Of this winter. Before dawn
It shifted a little and wetter. First light, the mist
Was like a nail in the head. She had gone through
Into the next field, but still lingered
Within close crying of her lamb, who lay now
Without eyes, already entrails pulled out
Between his legs. She cried for him to follow,
Now she felt so much lighter. As she cried
The two rams came bobbing over the hill,
The greyface and the blackface.
                                    They came straight on,
Noses stretching forward as if they were being pulled
By nose-rings. They milled merrily round her,
Fitting their awkward bodies to the requirement
That was calling, and that they could not resist
Or properly understand yet. Confusion of smells
And excitements. She ran off. They followed.
The greyface squared back and bounced his brow
Off the head of the surprised blackface, who stopped.
The greyface hurried on and now she followed.
He was leading her away and she followed.
She had stopped crying to her silent lamb.
The blackface caught them up on the steepness.
The greyface shouldered her away, drew back
Six or seven paces, dragging his forelegs, then curling
    his head.

He bounded forward and the other met him.
The blackface stood sideways. Then the greyface
Hurried to huddle with her. She hurried nibbling,
Making up for all she'd missed with her crying.
Then blackface came again. The two jostled her,
Both trying to mount her simultaneously
As she ran between them and under them
Hurrying to nibble further.
They drew back and bounced and collided again.
The greyface turned away as if
He'd done something quite slight but necessary
And mounted her as she nibbled. There he stayed.
The blackface ran at her and, baffled, paused.
Searched where to attack to get her for himself.
The greyface withdrew and flopped off,
And she ran on nibbling. The two rams
Turned to stare at me.
Two or three lambs wobbled in the cold.

10 March 1975

Ravens

As we came through the gate to look at the few new
  lambs
On the skyline of lawn smoothness,
A raven bundled itself into air from midfield
And slid away under hard glistenings, low and guilty.
Sheep nibbling, kneeling to nibble the reluctant
  nibbled grass.
Sheep staring, their jaws pausing to think, then
  chewing again,
Then pausing. Over there a new lamb
Just getting up, bumping its mother's nose
As she nibbles the sugar coating off it
While the tattered banners of her triumph swing and
  drip from her rear-end.
She sneezes and a glim of water flashes from her rear-
  end.
She sneezes again and again, till she's emptied.
She carries on investigating her new present and
  seeing how it works.
Over here is something else. But you are still
  interested
In that new one, and its new spark of voice,
And its tininess.
Now over here, where the raven was,
Is what interests you next. Born dead,
Twisted like a scarf, a lamb of an hour or two,
Its insides, the various jellies and crimsons and
  transparencies
And threads and tissues pulled out
In straight lines, like tent ropes

From its upward belly opened like a lamb-wool
      slipper,
The fine anatomy of silvery ribs on display and the
      cavity,
The head also emptied through the eye-sockets,
The woolly limbs swathed in birth-yolk and impossible
To tell now which in all this field of quietly nibbling
      sheep
Was its mother. I explain
That it died being born. We should have been here, to
      help it.
So it died being born. 'And did it cry?' you cry.
I pick up the dangling greasy weight by the hooves
      soft as dogs' pads
That had trodden only womb-water
And its raven-drawn strings dangle and trail,
Its loose head joggles, and 'Did it cry?' you cry again.
Its two-fingered feet splay in their skin between the
      pressures
Of my fingers and thumb. And there is another,
Just born, all black, splaying its tripod, inching its new
      points
Towards its mother, and testing the note
It finds in its mouth. But you have eyes now
Only for the tattered bundle of throwaway lamb.
'Did it cry?' you keep asking, in a three-year-old field-
      wide
Piercing persistence. 'Oh yes' I say 'it cried.'

Though this one was lucky insofar
As it made the attempt into a warm wind
And its first day of death was blue and warm
The magpies gone quiet with domestic happiness
And skylarks not worrying about anything

And the blackthorn budding confidently
And the skyline of hills, after millions of hard years,
Sitting soft.

15 April 1974

February 17th

A lamb could not get born. Ice wind
Out of a downpour dishclout sunrise. The mother
Lay on the mudded slope. Harried, she got up
And the blackish lump bobbed at her back-end
Under her tail. After some hard galloping,
Some manoeuvring, much flapping of the backward
Lump head of the lamb looking out,
I caught her with a rope. Laid her, head uphill
And examined the lamb. A blood-ball swollen
Tight in its black felt, its mouth gap
Squashed crooked, tongue stuck out, black-purple,
Strangled by its mother. I felt inside,
Past the noose of mother-flesh, into the slippery
Muscled tunnel, fingering for a hoof,
Right back to the port-hole of the pelvis.
But there was no hoof. He had stuck his head out too
    early
And his feet could not follow. He should have
Felt his way, tip-toe, his toes
Tucked up under his nose
For a safe landing. So I kneeled wrestling
With her groans. No hand could squeeze past
The lamb's neck into her interior
To hook a knee. I roped that baby head
And hauled till she cried out and tried
To get up and I saw it was useless. I went
Two miles for the injection and a razor.
Sliced the lamb's throat-strings, levered with a knife
Between the vertebrae and brought the head off
To stare at its mother, its pipes sitting in the mud
With all earth for a body. Then pushed

30

The neck-stump right back in, and as I pushed
She pushed. She pushed crying and I pushed gasping.
And the strength
Of the birth push and the push of my thumb
Against that wobbly vertebra were deadlock,
A to-fro futility. Till I forced
A hand past and got a knee. Then like
Pulling myself to the ceiling with one finger
Hooked in a loop, timing my effort
To her birth push groans, I pulled against
The corpse that would not come. Till it came.
And after it the long, sudden, yolk-yellow
Parcel of life
In a smoking slither of oils and soups and syrups –
And the body lay born, beside the hacked-off head.

17 February 1974

March morning unlike others

Blue haze. Bees hanging in air at the hive-mouth.
Crawling in prone stupor of sun
On the hive-lip. Snowdrops. Two buzzards,
Still-wings, each
Magnetized to the other,
Float orbits.
Cattle standing warm. Lit, happy stillness.
A raven, under the hill,
Coughing among bare oaks.
Aircraft, elated, splitting blue.
Leisure to stand. The knee-deep mud at the trough
Stiffening. Lambs freed to be foolish.

The earth invalid, dropsied, bruised, wheeled
Out into the sun,
After the frightful operation.
She lies back, wounds undressed to the sun,
To be healed,
Sheltered from the sneapy chill creeping North wind,
Leans back, eyes closed, exhausted, smiling
Into the sun. Perhaps dozing a little.
While we sit, and smile, and wait, and know
She is not going to die.

15 March 1974

Turning out

Turned the cows out two days ago.
Mailed with dung, a rattling armour,
They lunged into the light,
Kneeling with writhing necks they
Demolished a hill of soil, horning and
Scouring their skull-tops. They hurried
Their udders and their stateliness
Towards the new pasture. The calves lagged, lost,
Remembering only where they'd come from,
Where they'd been born and had mothers. Again
And again they galloped back to the empty pens,
Gazing and mooing and listening. Wearier, wearier –
Finally they'd be driven to their mothers,
Startling back at gates, nosing a nettle
As it might be a snake. Then
Finding their field of mothers and simple grass,
With eyes behind and sideways they ventured
Into the flings and headlong, breakthrough
Gallops toward freedom, high tails riding
The wonderful new rockinghorse, and circling
Back to the reassuring udders, the flung
Sniffs and rough lickings. The comforting
Indifference and contentment, which
They settled to be part of.

3 May 1975

She has come to pass

A whole day
Leaning on the sale-ring gates
Among the peninsula's living gargoyles,
The weathered visors
Of the labourers at earth's furnace
Of the soil's glow and the wind's flash,
Hearing the auctioneer's
Epic appraisal

Of some indigenous cattle, as if
This were the soul's timely masterpiece.
Comparing buttocks, anxious for birth-dates,
Apportioning credit for the calf,
Finally climaxing her blood-pressure
In a table-tennis to-fro strife

Of guineas by twenties for a bull
All of three quarters of a ton
Of peace and ability, not to say
Beauty, and to lose it, after all,
And to retire, relieved she had lost it, so,
As from a job well done.

30 May 1974

Birth of Rainbow

This morning blue vast clarity of March sky
But a blustery violence of air, and a soaked overnight
Newpainted look to the world. The wind coming
Off the snowed moor in the South, razorish,
Heavy-bladed and head-cutting, off snow-powdered
    ridges.
Flooded ruts shook. Hoof-puddles flashed. A daisy
Mud-plastered unmixed its head from the mud.
The black and white cow, on the highest crest of the
    round ridge,
Stood under the end of a rainbow.
Head down licking something, full in the painful wind
That the pouring haze of the rainbow ignored.
She was licking her gawky black calf
Collapsed wet-fresh from the womb, blinking his eyes
In the low morning dazzling washed sun.
Black, wet as a collie from a river, as she licked him,
Finding his smells, learning his particularity.
A flag of bloody tissue hung from her back-end
Spreading and shining, pink-fleshed and raw, it
    flapped and coiled
In the unsparing wind. She positioned herself, uneasy
As we approached, nervous small footwork
On the hoof-ploughed drowned sod of the ruined
    field.
She made uneasy low noises, and her calf too
With his staring whites, mooed the full clear calf-note
Pure as woodwind, and tried to get up,
Tried to get his cantilever front legs
In operation, lifted his shoulders, hoisted to his knees,
Then hoisted his back end and lurched forward

On his knees and crumpling ankles, sliding in the
    mud
And collapsing plastered. She went on licking him.
She started eating the banner of thin raw flesh that
Spinnakered from her rear. We left her to it.
Blobbed antiseptic on to the sodden blood-dangle
Of his muddy birth-cord, and left her
Inspecting the new smell. The whole South West
Was black as nightfall.
Trailing squall-smokes hung over the moor leaning
And whitening towards us, then the world blurred
And disappeared in forty-five degree hail
And a gate-jerking blast. We got to cover.
Left to God the calf and his mother.

19 March 1974

Orf

Because his nose and face were one festering sore
That no treatment persuaded, month after month,
And his feet four sores, the same,
Which could only stand and no more,

Because his sickness was converting his growth
Simply to strengthening sickness
While his breath wheezed through a mask of flies
No stuff could rid him of

I shot the lamb.
I shot him while he was looking the other way.
I shot him between the ears.

He lay down.
His machinery adjusted itself
And his blood escaped, without loyalty.

But the lamb-life in my care
Left him where he lay, and stood up in front of me

Asking to be banished,
Asking for permission to be extinct,
For permission to wait, at least,

Inside my head
In the radioactive space
From which the meteorite had removed his body.

3 July 1976

37

Happy calf

Mother is worried, her low, short moos
Question what's going on. But her calf
Is quite happy, resting on his elbows,
With his wrists folded under, and his precious hind legs
Brought up beside him, his little hooves
Of hardly-used yellow-soled black.
She looms up, to reassure him with heavy lickings.
He wishes she'd go away. He's meditating
Black as a mole and as velvety,
With a white face-mask, and a pink parting,
With black tear-patches, but long
Glamorous white eyelashes. A mild narrowing
Of his eyes, as he lies, testing each breath
For its peculiar flavour of being alive.
Such a pink muzzle, but a black dap
Where he just touched his mother's blackness
With a tentative sniff. He is all quiet
While his mother worries to and fro, grazes a little,
Then looks back, a shapely mass
Against the South sky and the low frieze of hills,
And moos questioning warning. He just stays,
Head slightly tilted, in the mild illness
Of being quite contented, and patient
With all the busyness inside him, the growing
Getting under way. The wind from the North
Marching the high silvery floor of clouds
Trembles the grass-stalks near him. His head wobbles
Infinitesimally in the pulse of his life.
A buttercup leans on his velvet hip.

He folds his head back little by breathed little
Till it rests on his shoulder, his nose on his ankle,
And he sleeps. Only his ears stay awake.

14 May 1975

Coming down through Somerset

I flash-glimpsed in the headlights – the high moment
Of driving through England – a killed badger
Sprawled with helpless legs. Yet again
Manoeuvred lane-ends, retracked, waited
Out of decency for headlights to die,
Lifted by one warm hindleg in the world-night
A slain badger. August dust-heat. Beautiful,
Beautiful, warm, secret beast. Bedded him
Passenger, bleeding from the nose. Brought him close
Into my life. Now he lies on the beam
Torn from a great building. Beam waiting two years
To be built into new building. Summer coat
Not worth skinning off him. His skeleton – for the
    future.
Fangs, handsome concealed. Flies, drumming,
Bejewel his transit. Heatwave ushers him hourly
Towards his underworlds. A grim day of flies
And sunbathing. Get rid of that badger.
A night of shrunk rivers, glowing pastures,
Sea-trout shouldering up through trickles. Then the
    sun again
Waking like a torn-out eye. How strangely
He stays on into the dawn – how quiet
The dark bear-claws, the long frost-tipped guard hairs!
Get rid of that badger today.
And already the flies.
More passionate, bringing their friends. I don't want
To bury and waste him. Or skin him (it is too late).
Or hack off his head and boil it
To liberate his masterpiece skull. I want him
To stay as he is. Sooty gloss-throated,

With his perfect face. Paws so tired,
Power-body relegated. I want him
To stop time. His strength staying, bulky,
Blocking time. His rankness, his bristling wildness,
His thrillingly painted face.
A badger on my moment of life.
Not years ago, like the others, but now.
I stand
Watching his stillness, like an iron nail
Driven, flush to the head,
Into a yew post. Something has to stay.

8 August 1975

Little red twin

Sister of little black twin,
Is sick. Scour. Granny, their mother,
For a change from pampering the herd's growthiest
   bullock,
Has this year preferred a pretty pair

Of miniature sisters. But her power-milk
Has overdone this baby's digestion who now,
Wobbly-legged, lags behind the migrations
From field-corner to corner. Her licked white face

Is still bravely calf-like, and does not
Comprehend the non-participation
Of her back-legs, or that huge drag-magnet
Of reluctance to move. Oh, she is sick!

She squirts yellow soup and waits.
Blue Dartmoor waits. The oak by the trough
Swirls its heat-wave shadow-skirt so slowly
It's half a day's sleep. Little red twin

Has to get her body here and there
On only quarter power. Now, one eighth power.
Examiners conclude, solemn,
She might not make it. Scour

Has drained her. She parches, dry-nosed.
We force-feed her with medical powder mix.
We brim her with pints of glucose water.
Her eyes are just plum softness, they thought

She'd come to be a cow. Dark-lovely
Eyes to attract protection. White eyelashes
To fringe her beauty that bit more perfect –
They have to go along with her failing.

And now after a day in the upper eighties
There she lies dead. The disc-harrow –
An intelligence test for perverse
Animal suicides – presented its puzzle,

And somehow she got her hind legs between bars
And fell as if cleverly forward, and locked
Where no mother could help her. There she lay
Up to eight hours, under the sun's weight.

As if to be sick-weak to the point of collapse
Had not been enough. Yet she's alive!

Extricated, slack as if limp dead,
But her eyes are watching. Her legs
Probably numb as dead. Her bleat
Worn to nothing. Just enough strength left

To keep her heart working, and her eye
Knowing and moist. Her mother
Had given her up and gone off. Now she comes back,
Clacks her ear tag, tack tack, on her horn,

Watches in still close-up, while we
Pump more glucose water down her daughter's
Helpless glug-glug. Sundown polishes the hay.
Propped on her crumpled legs, her sunk fire

Only just in. Now some sacks across her,
To keep in the power of the glucose

43

Through night's bare-space leakage. The minutes
Will come one by one, with little draughts,
And feel at her, and feel her ears for warmth,
And reckon up her chances, all night
Without any comfort. We leave her
To her ancestors, who should have prepared her

For worse than this. The smell of the mown hay
Mixed by moonlight with driftings of honeysuckle
And dog-roses and foxgloves, and all
The warmed spices of earth
In the safe casket of stars and velvet

Did bring her to morning. And now she will live.

1 June 1975

Teaching a dumb calf

She came in reluctant. The dark shed
Was too webby with reminiscences, none pleasant,
And she would not go in. She swung away
Rolled her tug belly in the oily sway of her legs.
Deep and straw-foul the mud. Leakage green
From earlier occupants, fermenting. I tried
To lift her calf in ahead of her, a stocky red block,
And she pacific drove her head at me
Light-nimble as a fist, bullied me off,
And swung away, calling her picky-footed boy
And pulling for the open field, the far beeches
In their fly-green emerald leaf of a day.
We shooed and shouted her back, and I tried again
Pulling the calf from among her legs, but it collapsed
Its hind legs and lay doggo, in the abominable mud,
And her twisting hard head, heavier than a shoulder,
Butted me off. And again she swung away.
Then I picked her calf up bodily and went in.
Little piggy eyes, she followed me. Then I roped her,
And drew her to the head of the stall, tightened her
Hard to the oak pillar, with her nose in the hay-rack,
And she choke-bellowed query comfort to herself.
He was trying to suck – but lacked the savvy.
He didn't get his nape down dipped enough,
Or his nose craning tongue upward enough
Under her tight hard bag of stiff teats each
The size of a labrador's muzzle. They were too big.
He nuzzled slobbering at their fat sides
But couldn't bring one in. They were dripping,
And as he excited them they started squirting.
I fumbled one into his mouth – I had to hold it,

45

Stuffing its slippery muscle into his suction,
His rim-teeth and working tongue. He preferred
The edge of my milk-lathered hand, easier dimension,
But he got going finally, all his new
Machinery learning suddenly, and she stilled,
Mooing indignity, rolling her red rims,
Till the happy warm peace gathered them
Into its ancient statue.

15 May 1975

Last load

Baled hay out in a field
Five miles from home. Barometer falling.
A muffler of still cloud padding the stillness.
The day after day of blue scorch up to yesterday,
The heavens of dazzling iron, that seemed unalterable,
Hard now to remember.

Now, tractor bounding along lanes, among echoes,
The trailer bouncing, all its iron shouting
Under sag-heavy leaves
That seem ready to drip with stillness.
Cheek in the air alert for the first speck.

You feel sure the rain's already started –
But for the tractor's din you'd hear it hushing
In all the leaves. But still not one drop
On your face or arm. You can't believe it.
Then hoicking bales, as if at a contest. Leaping
On and off the tractor as at a rodeo.

Hurling the bales higher. The loader on top
Dodging like a monkey. The fifth layer full
Then a teetering sixth. Then for a seventh
A row down the middle. And if a bale topples
You feel you've lost those seconds forever.
Then roping it all tight, like a hard loaf.

Then fast as you dare, watching the sky
And watching the load, and feeling the air darken
With wet electricity,
The load foaming through leaves, and wallowing

Like a tug-boat meeting the open sea –
The tractor's front wheels rearing up, as you race,
And pawing the air. Then all hands
Pitching the bales off, in under a roof,
Anyhow, then back for the last load.

And now as you dash through the green light
You see between dark trees
On all the little emerald hills
The desperate loading, under the blue cloud.

Your sweat tracks through your dust, your shirt flaps
    chill,
And bales multiply out of each other
All down the shorn field ahead.
The faster you fling them up, the more there are of
    them –
Till suddenly the field's grey empty. It's finished.

And a tobacco reek breaks in your nostrils
As the rain begins
Softly and vertically silver, the whole sky softly
Falling into the stubble all round you

The trees shake out their masses, joyful,
Drinking the downpour.
The hills pearled, the whole distance drinking
And the earth-smell warm and thick as smoke

And you go, and over the whole land
Like singing heard across evening water
The tall loads are swaying towards their barns
Down the deep lanes.

20 June 1975

While she chews sideways

He gently noses the high point of her rear-end
Then lower and on each side of the tail,
Then flattens one ear, and gazes away, then decidedly
    turns, wheels,
And moves in on the pink-eyed long-horned grey.
He sniffs the length of her spine, arching slightly
And shitting a tumble-thud shit as he does so.
Now he's testy.
He takes a push at the crazy galloway with the laid
    back ears.
Now strolling away from them all, his aim at the
    corner gate.
He is scratching himself on the fence, his vibration
Travels the length of the wire.
His barrel bulk is a bit ugly.
As bulls go he's no beauty.
His balls swing in their sock, one side idle.
His skin is utility white, shit-patched,
Pink sinewed at the groin, and the dewlap nearly
    naked.
A feathery long permed bush of silky white tail –
It hangs straight like a bell rope
From the power-strake of his spine.
He eats steadily, not a cow in the field is open,
His gristly pinkish head, like a shaved blood-hound,
Jerking at the grass.
Overmuch muscle on the thighs, jerk-weight settling
Of each foot, as he eats forward.
His dangle tassel swings, his whole mind
Anchored to it and now dormant.
He's feeding disgustedly, impatiently, carelessly.

49

His nudity is a bit disgusting. Overmuscled
And a bit shameful, like an overdeveloped body-
    builder.
He has a juvenile look, a delinquent eye
Very unlikeable as he lifts his nostrils
And his upper lip, to test a newcomer.
Today none of that mooning around after cows,
That trundling obedience, like a trailer. None of the
    cows
Have any power today, and he's stopped looking.
He lays his head sideways, and worries the grass,
Keeping his intake steady.

                                    15 September 1973

Sheep

The sheep has stopped crying.
All morning in her wire-mesh compound
On the lawn, she has been crying
For her vanished lamb. Yesterday they came.
Then her lamb could stand, in a fashion,
And make some tiptoe cringing steps.
Now he has disappeared.
He was only half the proper size.
And his cry was wrong. It was not
A dry little hard bleat, a baby-cry.
Over a flat tongue, it was human,
It was a despairing human smooth Oh!
Like no lamb I ever heard. Its hindlegs
Cowered in under its lumped spine,
Its feeble hips leaned towards
Its shoulders for support. Its stubby
White wool pyramid head, on a tottery neck,
Had sad and defeated eyes, pinched, pathetic,
Too small, and it cried all the time
Oh! Oh! staggering towards
Its alert, baffled, stamping, storming mother
Who feared our intentions. He was too weak
To find her teats, or to nuzzle up in under,
He hadn't the gumption. He was fully
Occupied just standing, then shuffling
Towards where she'd removed to. She knew
He wasn't right, she couldn't
Make him out. Then his rough-curl legs,
So stoutly built, and hooved

With real quality tips,
Just got in the way, like a loose bundle
Of firewood he was cursed to manage,
Too heavy for him, lending sometimes
Some support, but no strength, no real help.
When we sat his mother on her tail, he mouthed her
    teat,
Slobbered a little, but after a minute
Lost aim and interest, his muzzle wandered,
He was managing a difficulty
Much more urgent and important. By evening
He could not stand. It was not
That he could not thrive, he was born
With everything but the will –
That can be deformed, just like a limb.
Death was more interesting to him.
Life could not get his attention.
So he died, with the yellow birth-mucus
Still in his cardigan.
He did not survive a warm summer night.
Now his mother has started crying again.
The wind is oceanic in the elms
And the blossom is all set.

20 May 1974

II

The mothers have come back
From the shearing, and behind the hedge
The woe of sheep is like a battlefield
In the evening, when the fighting is over,
And the cold begins, and the dew falls,
And bowed women move with water.

Mother Mother Mother the lambs
Are crying, and the mothers are crying.
Nothing can resist that probe, that cry
Of a lamb for its mother, or a ewe's crying
For its lamb. The lambs cannot find
Their mothers among those shorn strangers.
A half-hour they have lamented,
Shaking their voices in desperation.
Bald brutal-voiced mothers braying out,
Flat-tongued lambs chopping off hopelessness
Their hearts are in panic, their bodies
Are a mess of woe, woe they cry,
They mingle their trouble, a music
Of worse and worse distress, a worse entangling,
They hurry out little notes
With all their strength, cries searching this way and
    that.
The mothers force out sudden despair, blaaa!
On restless feet, with wild heads.

Their anguish goes on and on, in the June heat.
Only slowly their hurt dies, cry by cry,
As they fit themselves to what has happened.

4 June 1976

The day he died

Was the silkiest day of the young year,
The first reconnaissance of the real spring,
The first confidence of the sun.

That was yesterday. Last night, frost.
And as hard as any of all winter.
Mars and Saturn and the Moon dangling in a bunch
On the hard, littered sky.
Today is Valentine's day.

Earth toast-crisp. The snowdrops battered.
Thrushes spluttering. Pigeons gingerly
Rubbing their voices together, in stinging cold.
Crows creaking, and clumsily
Cracking loose.

The bright fields look dazed.
Their expression is changed.
They have been somewhere awful
And come back without him.

The trustful cattle, with frost on their backs,
Waiting for hay, waiting for warmth,
Stand in a new emptiness.

From now on the land
Will have to manage without him.
But it hesitates, in this slow realization of light,
Childlike, too naked, in a frail sun,
With roots cut
And a great blank in its memory.

A monument

Your burrowing, gasping struggle
In the knee-deep mud of the copse ditch
Where you cleared, with bill-hook and slasher,
A path for the wire, the boundary deterrent,
That memorable downpour last-ditch hand to hand
    battle
With the grip of the swamped blue clay, to and fro,
The wallowing weight of the wire-roll,
Your raincoat in tatters, face fixed at full effort,
And the to-fro lurching under posts and tools and pile-
    driver,
While the rain glittered all the sapling purple birches
And clothing deadened to sheet lead,
That appalling stubbornness of the plan, among
    thorns,
Will remain as a monument, hidden
Under tightening undergrowth
Deep under the roadside's car-glimpsed May beauty,
To be discovered by some future owner
As a wire tensed through impassable thicket,
A rusting limit, where cattle, pushing unlikely,
Query for two minutes, at most,
In their useful life.
And that is where I remember you,
Skullraked with thorns, sodden, tireless,
Hauling bedded feet free, floundering away
To check alignments, returning, hammering the staple
Into the soaked stake-oak, a careful tattoo
Precise to the tenth of an inch,
Under December downpour, mid-afternoon
Dark as twilight, using your life up.

The formal auctioneer

Is trying to sell cattle. He is like a man
Walking noisily through a copse
Where nothing will be flushed. All eyes watch.
The weathered, rooty, bushy pile of faces,
A snaggle of faces
Like pulled-out and heaped-up old moots,
The natural root archives
Of mid-Devon's mud-lane annals,
Watch and hide inside themselves
Absorbing the figures like weather,
Or if they bid, bid invisibly, visit
The bidding like night-foxes,
Slink in and out of bidding
As if they were no such fools
To be caught interested in anything,
Escaping a bidding with the secret
Celebration of a bargain, a straight gain
And that much now in hand.

When you were among them
Hidden in your own bidding, you stood tall,
A tree with two knot-eyes, immovable,
A root among roots, without leaf,
Buying a bullock, with the eye-gesture
Of a poker-player
Dead-panning his hand. Deep-root weathering
The heat-wave of a bargain.

A memory

Your bony white bowed back, in a singlet,
Powerful as a horse,
Bowed over an upturned sheep
Shearing under the East chill through-door draught
In the cave-dark barn, sweating and freezing –
Flame-crimson face, drum-guttural African curses
As you bundled the sheep
Like tying some oversize, overweight, spilling bale
Through its adjustments of position

The attached cigarette, bent at its glow
Preserving its pride of ash
Through all your suddenly savage, suddenly gentle
Masterings of the animal

You were like a collier, a face-worker
In a dark hole of obstacle
Heedless of your own surfaces
Inching by main strength into the solid hour,
Bald, arch-wrinkled, weathered dome bowed
Over your cigarette comfort

Till you stretched erect through a groan
Letting a peeled sheep leap free

Then nipped the bud of stub from your lips
And with glove-huge, grease-glistening carefulness
Lit another at it

Now you have to push

Your hands
Lumpish roots of earth cunning
So wrinkle-scarred, such tomes
Of what has been collecting centuries
At the bottom of so many lanes
Where roofs huddle smoking, and cattle
Trample the ripeness

Now you have to push your face
So tool-worn, so land-weathered,
This patch of ancient, familiar locale,
Your careful little moustache,
Your gangly long broad Masai figure
Which you decked so dapperly to dances,
Your hawser and lever strength
Which you used, so recklessly,
Like a tractor, guaranteed unbreakable

Now you have to push it all –
Just as you loved to push the piled live hedge-boughs –
Into a gathering blaze

And as you loved to linger late into the twilight,
Coaxing the last knuckle embers,
Now you have to stay
Right on, into total darkness

Hands

Your hands were strange – huge.
A farmer's joke: 'still got your bloody great hands!'
You used them with as little regard
As old iron tools – as if their creased, glossed,
   crocodile leather
Were nerveless, like an African's footsoles.

When the barbed wire, tightening hum-rigid,
Snapped and leaped through your grip
You flailed your fingers like a caned boy, and laughed:
'Barbarous wire!' then just ignored them
As the half-inch deep, cross-hand rips dried.

And when your grasp nosed bullocks, prising their
   mouths wide,
So they dropped to their knees
I understood again
How the world of half-ton hooves, and horns,
And hides heedless as oaken-boarding, comes to be
   manageable.

Hands more of a piece with your tractor
Than with their own nerves,
Having no more compunction than dung-forks,
But suave as warm oil inside the wombs of ewes,
And monkey delicate

At that cigarette
Which glowed patiently through all your labours
Nursing the one in your lung

To such strength, it squeezed your strength to water
And stopped you.

Your hands lie folded, estranged from all they have
    done
And as they have never been, and startling –
So slender, so taper, so white,
Your mother's hands suddenly in your hands –
In that final strangeness of elegance.

Notes

page 3 Dehorning

That first year or two, we did all the jobs that required handling of the animals in a small yard. Twenty cows were all it could hold. Most cattle nowadays are dehorned soon after birth, but at that time many of the cows you bought still had horns. Among the unhorned, these soon discovered the point of power. So, in the end, they had to face what I describe here. As it happens, I made another note of the very same occasion, a different kind of observation, which now reminds me what a shattering effect the operation had on me, though I am not squeamish. As if the horns had been repeatedly sawn off me. The 'crush' is an adjustable steel cage for immobilizing a beast.

page 5 Poor birds

This next piece is a scrap of afterbirth from that first description of our labours in the winter rain. That winter, in particular, was doubly darkened – by bigger hordes of invading starlings than I had ever seen. All day long they would be storming down on to the field beside us, or roaring up, wired to every rumour, in a bewildered refugee panic, very disturbing, even slightly depressing, and somehow ominous, since they couldn't be ignored, and wherever you glanced you saw another tribe of starlings fleeing across the sky. Yet I was more touched by the redwings, who hurried about in smaller, quieter detachments, with secretive cries, the lost stragglers of an army rather than an army. These more diffident foreigners seemed by contrast much more aware of their plight, much more exposed to the ultimate fact: that this was all there was.

page 8 Foxhunt

The Reverend Jack Russell, the Victorian inventor of the Jack Russell terrier, was a fanatical foxhunter, who would and sometimes did hunt six days a week. When he came as Parson to Iddesleigh, a small village very close to the setting of this journal, foxhunting on horseback, to hounds, was unknown in the region, and he was dismayed to learn that there wasn't a single fox to be found between Dartmoor, seven miles to the south, and Torrington, eleven miles to the north, and the same distances to east and west. Every fox glimpsed in this territory was instantly reported, like a man-eater, and dug out and killed, by the farmers or by a commando of villagers. Jack Russell managed to interest two or three farmers in forming a hunt, and persuaded them to set down foxes in artificial dens and generally to protect them. More farmers became interested, and began to half-protect foxes. Pretty soon he had a thriving hunt going. The country people too, evidently, adjusted their feelings about foxes. Presumably they found themselves stirred by the ritual and ceremony of the hunt. Even after horses had passed out of common use, and that atavistic fear of what a man becomes when he gets up into the saddle had revived again, country folk still remained involved in the horse cult. Maybe because it is such a big part of the lives of girls and women (a girl or a woman on a horse is a different matter). The whole business is mysterious, but one consequence has been that the foxes of North Devon flourish in the most extraordinary way. They might well disapprove of my hard words against the houndpack. For all I know, they regard Jack Russell as their patron Saint. At a recent Meet starting from the Duke Of York in Iddesleigh, when the first little wood was drawn, just outside the village, foxes ran out in every direction. An explosion of foxes! The houndpack was completely bewildered. Observers reckoned 'over twenty foxes'.

page 19 Roe-deer

About two months after this encounter, I met one of these animals again (one of the same pair, I imagine) in a strange episode that sent me back to re-read my own verses. If those two deer, on that snowy February morning, had gone on downhill, and through the copse visible in the combe (the 'tree dark' from which they had probably started), they would have been stopped, at the bottom of the next field, by the River Taw. In April, I was standing beside that river just after dawn, and looking up the grassy combe, where the first rays of sun rested on the very heavy dew. In other words, I was looking up towards that copse I mention above. I suddenly realized I was being watched – by a figure outlined on the swell of the hill against the copse tucked in behind, a figure I took to be a man. When he started walking towards me I could see that he was unusually small, and somehow unnatural, but in what way unnatural I couldn't at that range quite make out. I kept perfectly still, and he approached me at a walk, so purposefully that I assumed he had seen me and wanted to speak to me. But the closer he came the odder he seemed. I had one of those moments, or rather several long moments, when you wonder whether what you are looking at actually is, at last, a ghost. At that hour in the morning I was ready for anything – certainly for a ghost. With those bright, rather brassy sunbeams full on him he looked absolutely solid and yet – unnatural: I could only think he must be some kind of earthy troll, some little old man living wild, or maybe even a little old woman. It was his confident approach, of course, that blocked the obvious. But my amazement hardly lessened when I realized that it was a roe-deer. It came the whole distance in a dead straight line. Till it stood, within twenty paces, clearly trying to puzzle out what kind of creature I might be, and thinking, perhaps, that I might be a big roe-buck. Then it circled to the left and studied me some more. Finally it turned and loped away up the field, stopping now and again to look back, till it paused, where I'd first seen it, looking back. Then it disappeared behind the hill.

page 34 She has come to pass

By the time we recoiled from the charms of foreign cattle breeds, we had settled our liking on South Devons. This was unorthodoxy. Every North Devon farmer's Bible states quite clearly that South Devon cattle cannot thrive 'north of the A 30' which runs, on its way from Penzance to Kensington, about six miles south of the farm. But we knew some of the best of the breed were much further north than that, and anyway we fancied them, even if only as a cross. So we set out to find a South Devon bull.

South Devons are generally reckoned the biggest native breed, but in fact they too are exotic. According to their history, they were introduced by Queen Eleanor, to supply beef and hides for the Fleet at Dartmouth, and came originally from the South of France. The main families still tend to be grouped around Dartmouth. We heard of a sale near Dartmouth where two or three quality bulls were being sold, and decided to go for one of them, a quite young animal, whose first calves were there to be admired. My wife bid – past our limit, past double our limit, and finally dropped out close to a figure three times our set limit. I left it too long before making a note, and so entirely missed the real point, which was our infatuation with that animal, and the wild relief at having escaped paying for him – exactly as if we had just won all that he had now cost somebody else. Nevertheless, the entry hangs on to something of the day, so I kept it.

page 35 Birth of Rainbow

What I sharply remember about this piece was how nearly I let it pass – like many another curious moment. That timing, the cow dropping the calf just as we set eyes on her (after we had watched her well into darkness the night before), was almost as peculiar as the fact that she gave birth under the end of a rainbow; and thinking about it that night I pushed myself out of bed to make the note, knowing that by the next day I would for sure have lost the authentic fingerprints of the day itself. I recall, too, how as I came to the close, Frost's line 'Something has to be left to God' strayed into my head, and how I made a quick bow around that, to tie the piece up. We called the calf Rainbow.

page 37 Orf

Small outbreaks of the ulcerous infection known as Orf or Lewer are fairly common among sheep and lambs. It generally begins around the lips and nose, but can spread anywhere (and can even make the leap on to the shepherd).

I missed the moment, here, by about two weeks. As I submitted to what seemed to be the requirements of the writing, I was keenly aware of all that I was rejecting. Details that were not important to the writing were still important to me! And still seem important. The lonely, hunched-up way he stood there, in the cattle pen, on

64

the lumpy, dry, compacted bedding (which was chicken litter from a battery farm – probably part of his failure to recover!), and the way the afternoon sun came on to him from the open opposite end of the building, and the shockingly-amplified crack of the rifle under the brittle asbestos roof. That should be there. And maybe the stony grave in the wood that I dug for him, and the little oak sapling that I planted on it (an extraordinary sort of funeral for any livestock casualty).

page 38 Happy calf

I sat close to this calf, where he sat on high ground, outlined against the bulk of Dartmoor six miles away, and I 'sketched' him in these words. I remember thinking, as his mother came between him and the blue shape of those hills. 'What a subject for an old Chinese painter!' This evoked the idea of a Chinese sage, on his mountain, in a trance, deep in Tao. The calf was obviously in a religious daze, the state of steady bliss which must be, one imagines, the normal mood of relaxing animals, their inborn defence against natural conditions. Our lost birthright. I kept all that from intruding with the single word 'meditating'.

page 42 Little red twin

The bulk of these pieces, I'm aware, concern the nursing if not the emergency hospital side of animal husbandry. All sheep, lambs and calves are patients: something in them all is making a steady effort to die. That is the farmer's impression. How many succeed is one of the things every farmer keeps to himself. On the other hand, the deepest fascination of stock rearing is this participation in the precarious birth of these tough and yet over-delicate beasts, and nursing them against what often seem to be the odds. 'Scour' is a chronic condition of diarrhoea, very common with young calves, usually fairly easy to cure, but debilitating while it lasts. Sometimes it ends in death. This occasion illustrated in an odd way what has always seemed to me almost a law: if anything can, even by only the remotest chance, operate as a trap, some animal will end up trapped in it.

page 45 Teaching a dumb calf

What I call the 'ancient statue' is simply the characteristic position that a calf takes up when it suckles, facing the opposite way to its mother, its upcurving back pressed close against the bulge of her belly, where she can reach round to give him a lick or a sniff. This makes a compact design, and appears in very early art.

page 49 While she chews sideways

The calf called Struggle, that died in one of the other pieces, was fathered by this bull, a colossal Charolais, a hired stud. Charolais bulls can be beautiful, but this one was not. Cows come into season about every twenty-one days. In a herd of thirty, the bull is always investigating. For the first month he lives through an ecstatic fugue of three-day infatuations, enthralled, even enslaved. Then as gaps begin to appear in the enchantment he becomes progressively more baffled and unbelieving.

page 51 Sheep I and II

Sometimes we brought an invalid in close to the house, where we could watch over it constantly. We would set up a small wire pen on the front lawn. On this occasion, we had brought in a ewe and her late-born, midget lamb – a lamb that had some quite special problem in staying alive, as well as being so unnaturally small. The following day, after he had gone, but before we had shifted his mother back to the flock, I made the note of Part I.

In Part II, I am being reminded of the first time I ever heard the uncanny noise that a large flock of sheep makes when the mothers, separated for the shearing from their still quite young lambs, return shorn – desperate to find the lambs that are desperate to find their mothers. There were no sheep on the South Yorkshire farms of my boyhood, and I had never heard a shearing on the moor farms of West Yorkshire either. During my National Service on an isolated RAF radio station I had the use of a powerful receiver, and through the night watches I could amuse myself searching the globe for the kind of music I liked. Late one night, roaming the space waves, I suddenly came into this unearthly lamentation, weaving and crackling through the galactic swells. I had no idea what it could be. I thought it must be, it had to be, the recording of the uproar on a battlefield, just after the attack. I listened for distinct words, or a stray gunshot or explosion. Then I thought it must be an inspired sound-effect for a radio version of Dante's Inferno, maybe an authentic battlefield recording used for a dramatization of Dante's descent, as all Hell opens beneath him. I listened for some explanation, but everything faded into a jabber of foreign commentary. The sound haunted me for two or three years, till I happened to walk in on a sheep-shearing on the moorland near Builth Wells. The flock was very large, and the lambs and their shorn, searching mothers were scattering over a wide valley. And there it was, in that empty landscape: my imagined battlefield, the outcry of the inferno.

On the occasion I record here, all the animals were very close to me, the other side of a high, thick hedge, in a field next to where I was working, so I could see nothing, only hear the sounds.

page 55 A monument

Farmers make especially valuable soldiers, I have read, because they are skilled in so many different ways. Jack Orchard belonged to that tradition of farmers who seem equal to any job, any crisis, using the most primitive means, adapting and improvising with any old bit of metal, and the more massive the physical demand, the more novel the engineering problem, the more intricate the mechanical difficulty, the better; and preferably the whole operation should be submerged under the worst possible weather. The concentration with which he transformed himself into these tasks, and the rapt sort of delight, the inner freedom, they seemed to bring him – all without a word spoken – gave me a new meaning for the phrase 'meditation on matter'. He made me understand how Stonehenge was hauled into place and set up as a matter of course, even if the great bluestones had to come from Limerick.

The episode I noted in 'A monument' brought this home to me because the job itself was such a very slight one – albeit so necessary and in those conditions so laborious – as tensing a strand of barbed wire through a wood. But it could have made no

67

difference to him, except maybe to intensify his satisfaction, if we had been doing it in the dark, or even under bombardment.

page 57 A memory

Throughout whatever he did, he smoked a cigarette. He rarely seemed to puff at it, just let it smoulder there. He spoke the broadest Devonshire with a very deep African sort of timbre. Unlike the indigenous Devonians who seem to be usually short, and often thick-set, he was very tall, broad and gangly, with immense hands. His line of Orchards came via Hartland, opposite the Isle of Lundy, which at one time was held by Moorish seafarers (hence the Moriscoes), and blood-group factors evidently do reveal pockets of North African genes here and there along the North and South Cornwall and Devon coasts. The Hartland Orchards have a crest: a raven. That could easily be accounted for, I used to tell him, if they had originally been Moorish pirates. We treat it as a joke, but for me it identified his essence.